PARADES

Senior Author
William K. Durr

Senior Coordinating Author
John J. Pikulski

Coordinating Authors
Rita M. Bean
J. David Cooper
Nicholas A. Glaser
M. Jean Greenlaw
Hugh Schoephoerster

Authors
Mary Lou Alsin
Kathryn Au
Rosalinda B. Barrera
Joseph E. Brzeinski
Ruth P. Bunyan

Jacqueline C. Comas
Frank X. Estrada
Robert L. Hillerich
Timothy G. Johnson
Pamela A. Mason
Joseph S. Renzulli

HOUGHTON MIFFLIN COMPANY   BOSTON

Atlanta   Dallas   Geneva, Illinois   Palo Alto   Princeton   Toronto

Acknowledgments

For each of the selections listed below, grateful acknowledgment is made for permission to adapt and/or reprint original or copyrighted material, as follows:

"Dogs," from *Around and About,* by Marchette Chute. Copyright © 1957 by Marchette Chute. Reprinted by permission of the author.

"Doghouse for Sale," from *Doghouse for Sale,* by Donna Lugg Pape. Copyright © 1979 by Donna Lugg Pape. Reprinted with the permission of Garrard Publishing Co., Champaign, Illinois.

"Ducks," from *Nuts to You and Nuts to Me,* by Mary Ann Hoberman. Copyright © 1974 by Mary Ann Hoberman. Reprinted by permission of Russell & Volkening, Inc. as agents for the author.

"Here Comes the Band," by William Cole. Copyright © 1960 by William Cole. Reprinted by permission of the author.

"The Hungry Fox," an adaptation of text of *The Hungry Fox and the Foxy Duck,* copyright © 1978 by Kathleen Leverich. A Parents Magazine Press Book. Reprinted by permission of E. P. Dutton, Inc. and William Heinemann Ltd.

Continued on page 237

Printed in the U.S.A.
ISBN: 0-395-43679-6

DEFGHIJ–D–943210–89

Contents

4

Parades
Magazine One

Contents

Stories

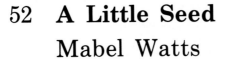

A Good Place to Play

by James Marshall

Some friends need a place to play.
Will they find one?

Dog: Stop! Stop that playing!

Cat: We can't stop playing, Dog.
We are going to be in a show.

Turtle: The show is tomorrow, Dog.
We want to be good.
So we have to play today.

Dog: That may be so.
But I'm trying to sleep!

Rabbit: It's daytime, Dog.
Why don't you sleep at night?

Dog: I have to work at night.

Cat: OK, Dog.
We'll go so that you can sleep.

Rabbit: Where will we go?
We have so much to do.
And we don't have much time!

Cat: I see a nice place.
Maybe we can play up there.

Turtle: Up there!
I can't get this thing up there.

Rabbit: Yes, you can, Turtle.
You can do it!

15

Turtle: I didn't think I would make it.
But this is a good place to play.

Cat: We can play all day and night!

Rabbit: We'll be so good tomorrow.
We'll be the best in the show.

Bear: Oh, no you will not!
I'm going to be the best.

Cat: We didn't see you, Bear!
What are you doing up here?

Bear: I have come here to sing.
And I can't sing when you play.
Please take your things and go.

Turtle: Some bears are no fun at all!

Hen: Cat! Turtle! Rabbit!
What a show we'll have tomorrow!

Cat: We can't be in the show, Hen.
We wouldn't be any good.

Rabbit: We didn't find a place to play.

Hen: Come with me, my friends.
I have a good place to play.
I'm on my way there now.

19

Cat: Now we can play all we want.

Rabbit: We'll be the best in the show!

Turtle: Things are looking up!

Summary Questions

The friends needed a place to play.
They did find a good place.
The questions will help you tell how.

1. Why did the friends need to play?
2. Some animals didn't want any playing. Why not?
3. How did the friends find a good place? Why was it the best place to play?
4. The friends are going to be in a show. Tell what you want the friends to play.

The Reading and Writing Connection

Cat   Turtle   Rabbit   Dog

Bear   Fox   Hen

What animals did you like best?

Are there any that you didn't like?

Tell why.

The words in the box may help you.

so	**night**	**way**
up	**sleep**	**when**

Here Comes the Band
by William Cole

The band comes booming
down the street,
The tuba oomphs,
the flutes tweet tweet;
The trombones slide,
the trumpets blare,
The baton twirls up in the air.
There are "ooh's!" and "ah's!"
and cheers and
clapping —
And I can't stop
my feet from tapping.

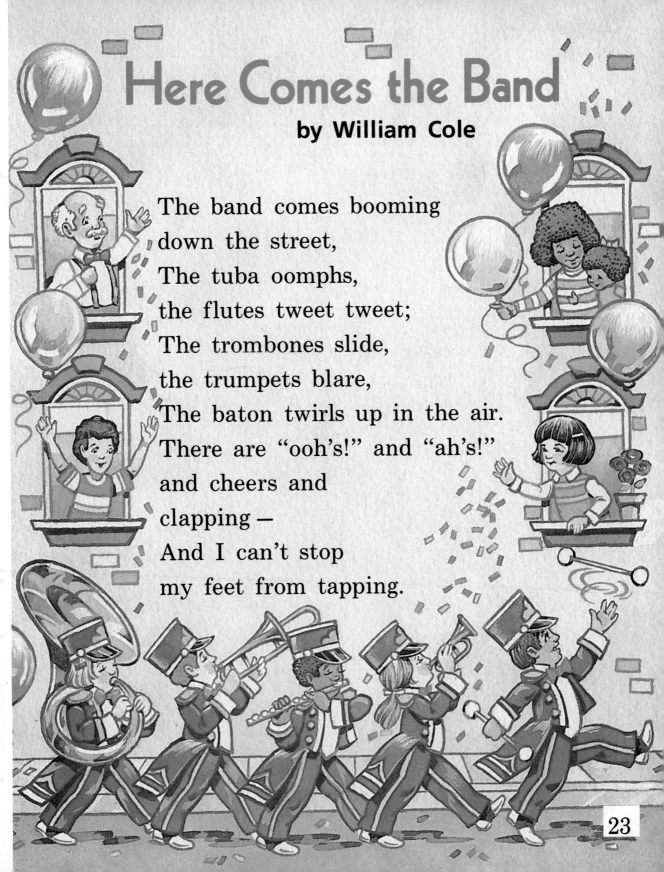

Alma's Idea

by Ann Míranda with María Guerrero

Alma needs a place to play.
Find out how she gets a place.

Lupe: You can't play in here, Alma!

Alma: Why not, Lupe?
This is my room, too.
Clara and I want
to play school.

Lupe: My friends and I
are playing in here now.
You and Clara are too little
to play with us.

Clara: We can play out here, Alma.

Alma: This isn't the best place
to play school, Clara.
But it will have to do.
Come on, let me see your book.
I'll help you to read a story.

Clara: Alma, look at this house.
It's in a tree!

Alma: That's a tree house, Clara.

Clara: It would be nice to have
a tree house.

Alma: Yes, it would be nice.
Then we would have
a place to play!

Clara: How can we have a tree house
when we don't have a tree?

Alma: I think I have an idea.

Clara: Show me your idea, Alma.

Alma: OK. What do you think?

Clara: It isn't like the tree house
in the story.
But it is a tree house!

Alma: I think my dad can help us.
I'll ask Dad now.

Alma: Dad, we need a place to play.
I have an idea for a tree house.
Would you help us make it?

Dad: I can help make the house,
but how can I make the tree?

Alma: Please look at my idea.
I think Mother can help us
with it, too.

Dad: It's a good idea, Alma!
Let's ask Mother now.

Alma: I want a tree house, Mother.
Dad is going to make the house.
Will you help make the tree?

Mother: How can we make a tree?

Dad: Take a look at Alma's idea.

Mother: Oh, now I see how.
Let's get to work.

Lupe:　What's going on down there?

Alma:　I need a place to play.
So Mother and Dad are helping me
to make a tree house!

Lupe:　A tree house?
You can't make a tree house
without a tree.

Alma:　Take a look at this!

Lupe: It *is* a tree house!
What a good idea, Alma.
Now when I play in our room,
you'll have a place to play.
Then when you want our room,
I'll play down here.

Alma: What a good idea, Lupe!

Summary Questions

Alma helped to make an idea
into something she wanted.

The questions will help you
tell how she did it.

1. Why wouldn't Lupe let Alma and Clara
   play in the room?
2. How did Alma get an idea for a place
   to play?
3. Did someone help Alma with the idea?
4. How did Alma get a tree house
   when she didn't have a tree?

The Reading and Writing Connection

Do you have an idea for a place
that you would like to make?

Where would it be?

Tell how you would make it.

Name the things you would need
to make it.

The words in the box may help you.

idea	room	dad
house	then	mother
	tree	ask

What Did They Say?

> I will help.
> I will.
> I will.

What did Hen say?
How can you tell she said it?

 I will help you, Rabbit.

 I would like help, Bear.

What did Bear say?
How can you tell he said it?

What did Rabbit say?
How can you tell he said it?

Alma: This is my room, too.

How can you tell that Alma said this?
The word **Alma** tells you.

Alma said, "This is my room, too."

How can you tell that Alma said this?
The words **Alma said** tell you.

"This is my room, too," said Alma.

Now how can you tell that Alma said this?
The words **said Alma** tell you.

Now read this story.

Ben said, "Look at my rabbit."

Amy said, "Oh, I like it."

"Can that rabbit help you
to swim?" asked Amy.

Ben said, "I'll make
the rabbit big.
Then it will help me to swim."

"Isn't that rabbit too big?"
asked Amy.

"It isn't too big," said Ben.
"I like big, big rabbits."

Ben said, "Oh, no!
What will we do now?"

"It's OK," said Amy.
"My turtle can help us to swim.
But I will not make my turtle
too big!"

The Little Red Hen

The little red hen is going
to make bread.
Who will get some bread?

One day the little red hen said,
"Come see what I have!
I have some wheat.
I am going to plant it."

"Who will help me plant the wheat?"
asked the little red hen.

"Not I," said the duck.

"Not I," said the cat.

"Not I," said the pig.

"Then I will plant it myself,"
said the little red hen.
And she did.

The wheat grew and grew.
It grew into big plants.

"Who will help me cut the wheat?" asked the little red hen.

"Not I," said the duck.

"Not I," said the cat.

"Not I," said the pig.

"Well then, I will cut it myself," said the little red hen.
And she did.

"Who will help me pound the wheat?" asked the little red hen.

"Not I," said the duck.

"Not I," said the cat.

"Not I," said the pig.

"Well then, I will pound it myself," said the little red hen.
And she did.

"I will take the wheat to the mill," said the little red hen.

"The mill will make the wheat into flour.

Who will help me take the wheat to the mill?"

"Not I," said the duck.

"Not I," said the cat.

"Not I," said the pig.

"Well then, I will take it myself," said the little red hen.
And she did.

"I will make bread with the flour,"
said the little red hen.
"Who will help me make the bread?"

"Not I," said the duck.

"Not I," said the cat.

"Not I," said the pig.

"Then I will make the bread myself,"
said the little red hen.
And she did.

"Now who will help me eat the bread?" asked the little red hen.

"I will," said the duck.

"I will," said the cat.

"I will," said the pig.

"Oh, no," said the little red hen.

"You did not help me plant the wheat.

You did not help me cut the wheat.

You did not help me pound the wheat.

You did not help me take the wheat
to the mill.

You did not help me make the bread,
so you will not help me eat the bread.

I am going to eat it myself."

And she did.

Summary Questions

The little red hen worked hard to make some bread.

The duck and the cat and the pig didn't get any bread.

The questions will help you tell why.

1. Who did all the work to make bread?
2. Who didn't do any work? Why not?
3. Who was the one to eat the bread?
4. Would you have let the animals help eat the bread? Why?
5. Think about all the things that the little red hen did to make bread. Then make a picture to show one thing she did.

The Reading and Writing Connection

In this story, no one helped
the little red hen.

Tell one more story about
the little red hen.

In your story, have all the animals
helping to make bread.

The words in the box can help you.

plant	**cut**	**wheat**	**bread**
eat	**mill**	**grew**	**pound**

A Little Seed

by Mabel Watts

A little seed
For me to sow . . .

A little earth
To make it grow . . .
A little hole,
A little pat . . .
A little wish,
And that is that.

A little sun,
A little shower . . .
A little while,
And then — a flower!

Pam and Lee Bake Bread

Pam and Lee are going
to make bread.

They can make the bread look
like a fish.

They can make it look like a bear.

Maybe they will make it look
like a turtle.

Let's see what Pam and Lee will do.

Pam and Lee mix some things like this.

They need to mix the things to make bread dough.

Then Pam and Lee mix the dough like this.

Pam and Lee put the dough
in a good place.

They'll keep it there for some time.

Soon the dough will get big.

Now Pam and Lee work
with the dough.

Look, they have a turtle bread!

It's time to bake the bread.
Pam will put it in to bake.
Soon there will be bread to eat.

Now Pam will cut the bread,
and she and Lee will eat some.
They'll eat some now
and keep the rest for tomorrow.

Summary Questions

The questions will help you tell what Pam and Lee did to make bread.

1. What things did Pam and Lee need?
2. How did they mix the dough?
3. Name the things Pam and Lee did. Start with the mixing, and keep going. Tell what they did with the bread.

The Reading and Writing Connection

Which animal would you make? Make a picture to show what your bread animal would look like. Tell what you would do with it. The words in the box may help you.

mix	bake	dough	keep

One More Thing, Dad

by Susan L. Thompson

Caleb is going for a walk.
Count the things Caleb will take
on the walk.

"I'm going out for a walk, Dad,"
Caleb said.

"Oh?" said Dad.

He was making bread.

"May I take a big orange with me?"
asked Caleb.

"There you are, Caleb," said Dad.
"There's an orange."

Caleb said, "That's 1."
He liked to count.

"Do you want something more?"
asked Dad.

"Maybe I'll take a sandwich, too,"
said Caleb.

"OK," said Dad.
"You can make it yourself."

Caleb liked making the sandwich.
Then he said, "That's 2."

"Some juice would be good
with this sandwich," said Caleb.

"Help yourself," said Dad.

"That's 3," Caleb counted.
"Now I'll get my lunch box," he said.

Caleb put the orange, the sandwich,
and the juice into the lunch box.
"This lunch box makes 4," he said.

"Now I'll need my jar," Caleb said.

"I think it's in your room," Dad said.

Caleb went to get the jar.
"It *was* there, Dad," said Caleb.
"That's 5," he counted.

"Now I'll need a coat," said Caleb.
"What do you think, Dad?"

Dad said, "Take your red coat."

Caleb went to get the red coat.
"6," he counted.
Then he said, "Maybe Obie
would like to come with me."

"Why not?" said Dad.
"Take Obie, too!"

"Obie! Come here, Obie," said Caleb.
"Obie makes 7," Caleb said to Dad.

Then Caleb went to get a kite.
"My kite will make 8," he said.
"And may I put on your hat, Dad?"

"It's yours!" said Dad, and he helped
Caleb put it on.

"9!" said Caleb.
"Now I have 9 things to take with me."

Caleb said, "I have an orange,
a sandwich, juice, my lunch box, my jar,
my coat, Obie, my kite, and your hat.
I think I have what I need.
I'm going out now."

"Have a good walk," Dad said.

But Caleb didn't go out.
He counted,
"1, 2, 3, 4, 5, 6, 7, 8, 9 . . ."

"What is it, Caleb?" Dad asked.

"One more thing, Dad," said Caleb.
"Will *you* come for a walk with me?"

"Why, Caleb, I would like to go
with you!" said Dad.

"Then you make 10, big, big 10!"
said Caleb.
"1, 2, 3, 4, 5, 6, 7, 8, 9, 10!"

Summary Questions

The questions will help you
tell what Caleb did for fun.

1. Do you think that Caleb likes to count?
   Why do you think that?
2. What did Caleb take on the walk?
   Count the things.
3. Why do you think Caleb wanted
   to take Dad on the walk?
4. Name some more things for Caleb
   to take on the walk.
   Now count all of the things
   you have named.

The Reading and Writing Connection

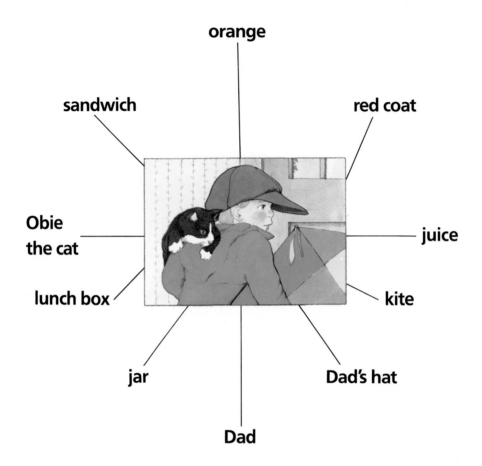

orange

sandwich

red coat

Obie
the cat

juice

lunch box

kite

jar

Dad's hat

Dad

The words name all of the things
Caleb wanted to take on the walk.

Make pictures to show what you think
he will do with the things.

Tell about your pictures.

71

Magazine Wrap-up

What Happened?

1. Alma, Pam and Lee, and Caleb
   all made some things.
   Tell what things they made.

2. Cat, Turtle, and Rabbit looked
   for a place to play.
   What kind of playing did they do?
   Alma wanted a place to play, too.
   What kind of playing will she do?

Help!

The little red hen didn't get help when she needed it, but Alma did.

Tell about a time when someone helped you.

Books to Enjoy

Apple Tree! Apple Tree!
by Mary Blocksma

See what a good friend an apple tree can be.

Are You My Mother? by P. D. Eastman

A baby bird falls from his nest.
Can he find his mother?

Go Away, Dog by Joan L. Nödset

How will a dog make friends
with a little boy?

74

Parades
Magazine Two

Contents

Doghouse for Sale

by Donna Lugg Pape

Freckles is going to put
a house up for sale.
Find out who will live
in it.

Freckles looked at his house.

"I don't want this house," he said.
"I will put this one up for sale."

Freckles put up a sign.

Dogs came to look at the house.
But no one wanted it.

"It needs paint," one dog said.

"Then I'll paint my house,"
said Freckles.
"I'll paint it red.
Then someone will want it."

Freckles went to the store
to get paint.
Then he went home.

Soon the house was painted red.
"That looks good," Freckles said.

Then Freckles put up a new sign.

Dogs came to look at the house.
But no one wanted it.

One dog said, "Your house needs a new bed."

"I'll make a new bed for my house," said Freckles.
"Then someone will want it."

So Freckles went back to the store to get what he needed to make a bed.

Soon the house had a new bed.

Freckles put up a new sign.

Dogs came to look at the house.
But no one wanted it.

One dog said, "It needs a window."

"I'll make a window for my house,"
said Freckles.
"Then someone will want it."

Freckles went back to the store.

Freckles worked hard.
Soon his house had a window.

Freckles put up a new sign.

Dogs came to look at the house.
But no one wanted it.

"Your house needs trees around it,"
one dog said.

"Then I'll plant some," said Freckles.

Freckles went back to the store
to get some trees.

Soon the house had trees around it.

Freckles put up a new sign.

Dogs came to look at the house.
"We like your house," the dogs said.
"All it needs is a fence around it."

So Freckles went back to the store
to get a fence.

Then he went home and put
the fence around his house.

Freckles put up a new sign.

Dogs came to look at the house.
"This is a good house," one dog said.
"I want to live in it."

Freckles walked around his house.

He looked at the red paint.

He looked at the window.

He looked at all the trees.

He looked at the fence around it.

"This house is not for sale,"
Freckles said.

"I want to live in it myself."

And he did.

Summary Questions

Freckles needed to do some things to his house.

The questions will help you tell why.

1. What did Freckles want to do with his house?
2. Why did he keep doing things to his house?
3. Why did he make new signs?
4. Tell why Freckles liked his house so much that he wanted to keep it.

The Reading and Writing Connection

Think like Freckles.

Tell a friend what new thing
you like best about your house.

Draw a picture of it.

Tell why you like that thing the best.

The words in the box may help you.

new	paint	sign	window
	fence	trees	live

Dogs

by Marchette Chute

The dogs I know
Have many shapes.
For some are big and tall,
    And some are long,
    And some are thin,
    And some
    are fat
    and small.

And some are little bits
    of fluff
And have no shape at all.

Signs All Around

There are signs all around you.
Some signs tell what to do,
while some signs tell what not to do.

Signs can tell you that no one
is in.

Signs can tell you that something
is for sale.

Signs can help you find your way.
They can tell you which way to go.
Here are some street signs.

Let's say you want to go to New Street.
Which one of the street signs tells you
the way to go?

When you go for a walk,
you may see signs like these.
   Some of the signs have words,
while other signs do not need words.
   What do these signs tell you?

You can make signs to tell things.
You can make some signs
with words, and others without words.

Summary Questions

These questions will help you tell about signs.

1. What are some things that signs can tell you?
2. Where do you find signs?
3. Tell about some signs you see all the time.
   What do these signs tell you?

The Reading and Writing Connection

Make two new signs.
Make one sign with words.
Make the other sign without words.
Then tell about your signs.

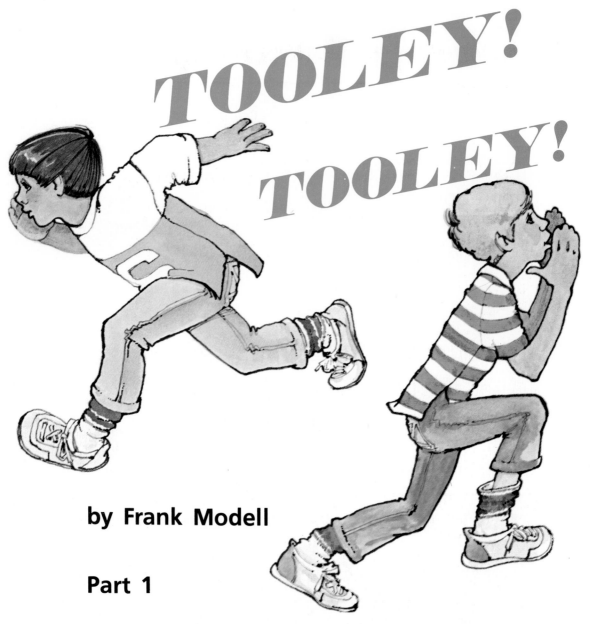

TOOLEY! TOOLEY!

by Frank Modell

Part 1

Marvin and Milton want to find
a brown dog.
See what they do to find the dog.

Marvin and Milton liked going
to the movies.

But on this day they had no money.

"Let's look around," said Marvin.
"Maybe we'll find some money."

Then Marvin said, "Look at
this sign."

"If we can find that dog, we'll have some money," said Marvin.

"I don't think we can find Tooley," said Milton.

"There are brown dogs all over the place."

"If I could fly, I could find Tooley,"
said Marvin.

"I would fly all over the place
and call for Tooley.

Tooley would look up and see me.

Then I would go down
and get Tooley."

"That's silly," said Milton.

"You don't like my ideas,"
said Marvin.

"I like your ideas when they
aren't silly," said Milton.

Then Marvin asked, "What if we
run up and down the street
and call for Tooley?

If I go this way, and you go
that way, one of us will find Tooley."

"We'll have to run," said Milton,
"if we want to see a movie."

So Marvin ran up the street
and Milton ran down the street.
They ran all around calling,
"Tooley! Tooley!"

Summary Questions

The questions will help you tell what Marvin and Milton did to find Tooley.

1. Why did the boys want to find Tooley?
2. What silly idea did Marvin have?
3. What other idea did Marvin have? Was it a good idea? Why?
4. Tell more ideas for finding Tooley. Think of silly ideas and good ones.

The Reading and Writing Connection

You could help the boys find Tooley. Draw a place where dogs would go. The words can help you tell about it.

| could | silly | brown | over | home |

TOOLEY! TOOLEY!

by Frank Modell

Part 2

Will Marvin and Milton find Tooley?
Will they have money for the movies?

Milton stopped and looked over
a fence.

There was a brown dog!

"Tooley?" asked Milton.
"You are Tooley, aren't you?
Tooley, I'm taking you home."

But then Milton saw a brown dog
on the street.

"I'll take him, too," Milton said.
"Maybe he is Tooley."

Marvin had found no dogs at all.
"If I were Tooley, where would
I go?" he asked himself.

Then it came to him.
"I would go
to Mr. Klopmeyer's store!"

"Mr. Klopmeyer," said Marvin,
"I'm looking for a dog."

"A hot dog?" asked Mr. Klopmeyer.

"No, not a hot dog!" said Marvin.
"That's silly!"

"Go take a look in the back,"
said Mr. Klopmeyer.
"You'll find some dogs out there."

Marvin looked at all the dogs.
"Tooley?" he asked.
A little brown dog ran up to him.

"You are Tooley!" said Marvin.
"I know you are!
Come on, Tooley.
You are going home."

"Tooley! Oh, Tooley!" said Lisa.
"Where were you?"

Marvin said, "I found him
at Mr. Klopmeyer's store."

Then Lisa said, "Thank you
for finding him.
This money is for you."

"Thanks," said Marvin.
"See you."

Then Marvin saw Milton running
down the street with some brown dogs.
"I found Tooley!" Milton called.

But then Milton saw that Marvin
had some money.

He could tell that Marvin
had found Tooley.

"I'll have to take back these dogs,"
Milton said.

"I'll help you," said Marvin.
"But we'll have to run all the way
if we want to get to the movies."

Summary Questions

The boys did many things
to find Tooley.

These questions will help you
tell how they found the dog.

1. Milton found many dogs.
   Why did he think that any
   of the dogs could be Tooley?
2. Why did Marvin think that Tooley
   could be at Mr. Klopmeyer's store?
3. Someday the boys may have to find
   another dog.
   What things will they think about?

The Reading and Writing Connection

The sign about Tooley was not
a big help to the boys.

What other things could the sign say?

Make a new sign.

Put all the things you know
about Tooley in your sign.

The words in the box will help you.

know	**eat**	**like**	**found**
tail	**little**	**brown**	**saw**

The Hungry Fox

by Kathleen Leverich

Fox is hungry.
He wants to eat Duck.
Will Fox eat Duck?

Once there was a smart little duck.
She lived on a pond.
The pond had a fence all around it.
It was good living on the pond.

One day the little duck saw
a hungry red fox.

"Come have breakfast with me,"
Fox called to Duck.

Duck looked at Fox.
"This fox is hungry," she thought.
"He looks hungry for ducks."

So Duck asked, "How can we
eat breakfast without a table?"

"Wait there," called Fox.
"I will get a table."

Fox ran and ran.
He jumped over the fence.

Soon Fox came to a house.

He looked in the window.

No one was home, but he saw
a little table.

"No one needs this table now,"
thought Fox.

"I will take it."

The fox ran back to the pond with the fence all around it.

"Here is a table," called Fox. "Come have breakfast with me, Duck."

"But I have had breakfast," called the little duck. "Soon it will be lunchtime."

"Then come have lunch with me,"
called Fox.

He was hungry for duck
after all that running.

Duck said, "I need a plate
to put my lunch on.
How can we eat without plates?"

"Wait there," called Fox.
"I will get plates."

Fox ran and ran.

Soon he came to a house.

No one was home, but Fox saw
some plates on a table.

"I need plates," thought Fox.
"I will take what I need."

Then the fox ran back to the pond with the fence around it.

"Here are the plates," called Fox. "Come have lunch with me, Duck."

"I have had lunch," said Duck. "Soon it will be supper time."

"Well then, come have supper
with me," called Fox.

He was so hungry for duck
after all that running.

The little duck asked, "How can
we eat supper without a tablecloth?"

"If I get a tablecloth, *then* will you
eat supper with me?" asked Fox.

"Yes," said Duck.

123

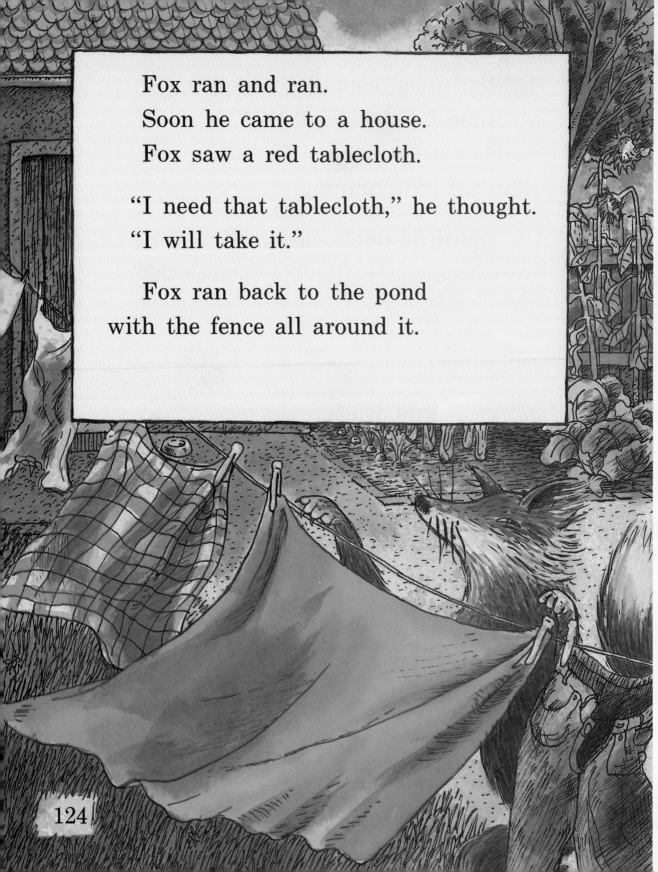

Fox ran and ran.
Soon he came to a house.
Fox saw a red tablecloth.

"I need that tablecloth," he thought.
"I will take it."

Fox ran back to the pond
with the fence all around it.

"Here's a tablecloth," called Fox.
"Come for supper, Duck."

"I want to see the tablecloth, Fox,"
called the smart little duck.
"I think it is too little."

"It's not too little," said Fox.
"Look!"

Then Fox saw why the pond
had a fence all around it.

Fox ran and ran,
and he didn't come back.

So once more it was good living
on the pond with the fence all around it.

Story Wrap-up

Summary Questions

Fox wanted to eat Duck, but he couldn't do it.

These questions will help you tell why.

1. Why didn't Fox have Duck for breakfast?
2. Why didn't Fox have Duck for lunch?
3. Why didn't Fox have Duck for supper?
4. Do you think Duck is smart? Why?

The Reading and Writing Connection

Tell about another place where
the hungry fox could go to eat.

What will Fox do if he goes there?

Will he think of any new ways
to get something to eat?

Start your story with the words
Once there was a hungry fox.

The words in the box may help you.

breakfast	**lunch**	**supper**
thought	**wait**	**hungry**
tablecloth	**after**	**pond**

Ducks

by Mary Ann Hoberman

Ducks are lucky,
Don't you think?
When they want to
Take a drink,
All they do is
Duck their bill.
(Doesn't matter
If they spill.)
When they want to
Take a swim,
All they do is
Dive right in;
And they never
Seem to sink.
Ducks are lucky,
Don't you think?

Vowels a, e, i, and o

Vowels You Know

You know two sounds
for the vowel **a.**

Look at the words in the box.

Say the words and think about
the vowel sounds.

short a

back	made
name	
had	ran

long a

Which words in the box
have a short **a** sound?

Which words have a long **a** sound?

You know two sounds
for the vowel **e** and two sounds
for the vowel **i.**

Say the words in each box.
Listen for the vowel sound
in each word.

short e

these	**keep**
let	
best	**well**

long e

Which words have a short **e** sound?
Which words have a long **e** sound?

short i

while	**swim**
if	
time	**like**

long i

Which words have a short **i** sound?
Which words have a long **i** sound?

Another vowel sound that you know
is the short **o** sound.

It is the vowel sound in **hot**.

Which of these things have names
with the short **o** sound?

The Long o Sound

Now say the word **go**.

The vowel sound in **go**
is the long **o** sound.

So, **home**, and **go** all have
the long **o** sound.

Which of these things have
names with the long **o** sound?

Say the words in the box.
Listen for the vowel sound
in each word.

short o

box	**nose**
home	
no	**not**

long o

Which words have a short **o** sound?
Which words have a long **o** sound?

Now you know the short
and the long **o** sounds.
Read what is in this box.

1. I will read the **note**.
2. Give me the **mop**, please.
3. Did you **drop** your hat?
4. John will tell a **joke**.

My Dog and the Key

by David A. Adler

Jennie thinks My Dog can find
lost things.
See if she can find a lost key.

My name is Jennie.

This is my dog.

I couldn't think of a good name
for her, so I named her My Dog.

My Dog is smart.

She can find lost things.

One day, My Dog and I
were by a tree.
We sat by the tree
for a long time.
It was a hot day.
But it was not hot by the tree.

My Dog pushed me with her nose.
She wanted me to take her
for a walk.

"Not now," I said.
"It's too hot."

My Dog pushed me some more,
but I still sat.

We were still at the tree
when Susan came by.

"I lost the key to my house!"
said Susan.
"My mother gave it to me today.
She said I am big now,
so I can have a key for myself.
But I lost it."

My Dog pushed me with her nose.

She wanted me to ask Susan more about the key.

So I asked her.

"I was in my house when my mother gave me the key," Susan said.

"But I don't know what I did with it."

This time I didn't wait for My Dog to poke me.

"Take us to your house," I said.

"My Dog will find the lost key."

Soon we were at Susan's house.

Susan said, "I was here
when my mother gave me the key.
But now I know that I didn't
put the key down.
I had it when I went up to my room."

We went up to Susan's room.

Her things were all over the place.

I didn't want My Dog to go in there.

I didn't want her to get lost.

Susan said, "Now I know I didn't
put my key down in here.

I had it when I went to the kitchen."

My Dog poked me with her nose.

"Let's go to the kitchen," I said.

Things were all over the kitchen.

"I was making biscuits," said Susan.
"I put the key here on the table."

There was no key on the table.

"Where did you roll out
the biscuit dough?" I asked.

"Here on the table," Susan said.

I started to think.

I thought about the key
and the biscuit dough.

"Oh, no!" said Susan.

My Dog was eating the biscuits.

"Stop it, My Dog!" Susan said.
"Stop eating all my biscuits."

"I know where your key is," I said.

"The key was on the table when you rolled out the dough," I said.

"You rolled the key up with the dough.

My Dog knows that.

She's eating your biscuits to find the key."

Susan didn't think My Dog wanted to find her key.

She thought My Dog was hungry.

But then we saw the key!

It fell out of a biscuit that My Dog
was eating.

It fell onto the table.

Susan thanked me for finding her key.

"Don't thank me," I said.
"Thank My Dog."

Susan started to thank My Dog,
but My Dog didn't look up.
She was still eating.

Summary Questions

Jennie and My Dog helped Susan find the lost key.

These questions will help you tell how they did it.

1. Where did Susan, Jennie, and My Dog go to look for Susan's key? How did going to each place help find the key?

2. Do you think Jennie and Susan would have found the key without My Dog? Why?

3. What do you think Jennie and My Dog would do to help Susan find her key if she lost it again?

The Reading and Writing Connection

Make a big picture of Susan's kitchen.
Now make a picture of a key
and put Susan's name on it.
Cut out the key you made.
Where would you put Susan's key
so that it would not get lost?
Put the key in that place
on your picture.
Tell why you put it there.
The words in the box can help you.

key	**by**	**kitchen**
	biscuit	**roll**

Action Words

Tricks and Jolly play.
They run and jump.

Read these words.
play   run   jump

The words **play, run,** and **jump** tell
what Tricks and Jolly do.

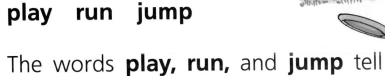

Tricks ———— dog biscuits.
   hats   eats
Which word tells what Tricks does?

Jolly ———— over.
   rolls   boys
Which word tells what Jolly does?

149

Magazine Wrap-up

Looking Back

1. Duck, Marvin, and Jennie each worked out a problem. Tell about each problem and how it was worked out.

2. Jennie said that My Dog was smart. Do you think My Dog was smart? Why? Was Freckles a smart dog? Why? How about Tooley? Why?

I Would Like to Play With ____

Think about Jennie, Susan, Marvin, and Milton.

Which one would you like to play with? Why?

Books to Enjoy

Harriet Reads Signs and More Signs
by Betsy and Giulio Maestro

Signs help Harriet find her way all around town.

Roll Over by Merle Peek

Some animals get in a bed one by one until there are too many!

Beware of a Very Hungry Fox
by Patty Wolcott

A hungry fox scares four chipmunks.

Parades
Magazine Three

153

Contents

Stories

Play

Willaby

by Rachel Isadora

Willaby gives a drawing
to Miss Finney, but she forgets
to sign it.
Will Miss Finney know who made
the drawing?

Willaby likes school.

She likes reading and counting.

She likes lunchtime.

She likes the children in her room.

She likes Miss Finney.

But Willaby likes to draw best.

When Miss Finney lets the children
decide what they want to do,
Willaby draws.

At home Willaby draws, too.

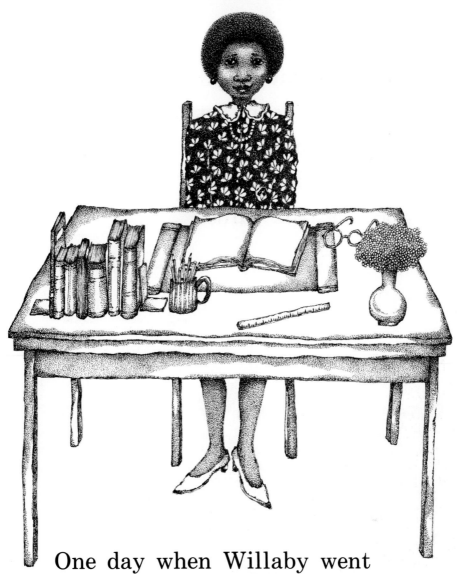

One day when Willaby went
to school, Miss Finney was sick.

Mrs. Benjamin said that Miss Finney
wouldn't be back to school for a while.

So the children decided to make
get-well cards for Miss Finney.

Then the children decided
to make up a poem for Miss Finney.
Mrs. Benjamin helped the children.
Soon the children were putting
the poem on the cards.

But not Willaby.
Willaby was drawing a picture.

Then Mrs. Benjamin asked
the children to give her the cards.
Willaby didn't know what to do.
She had not made a get-well card
for Miss Finney.
Now there was no time to make one.

Willaby decided to give her drawing
to Miss Finney.

On her way home that day,
Willaby thought, "I didn't put
my name on my drawing!
Now Miss Finney will not know
that I made something for her.
She may think I don't like her."

162

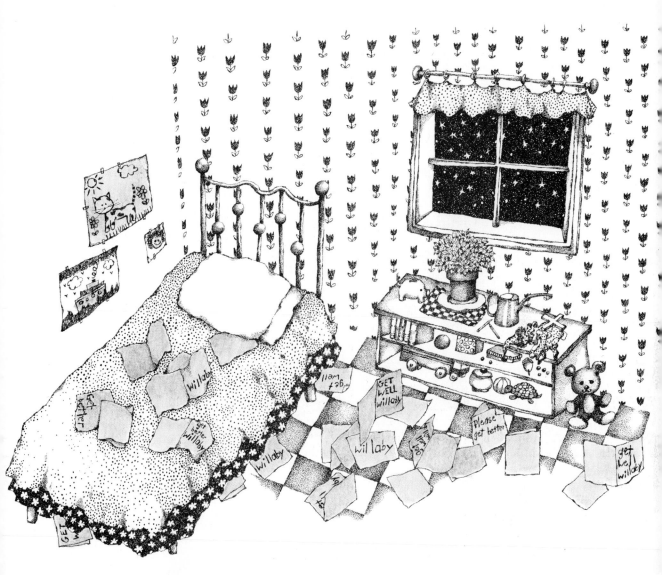

All the time that Miss Finney
was sick, Willaby made many cards
for her.

Willaby signed all the cards.

Soon it was the day for Miss Finney
to come back to school.

Willaby didn't want to go
to school that day.

She decided to take her time
and walk there.

At school, Willaby walked over
to her table without looking
at Miss Finney.

Then Willaby saw something
on her table.

Willaby didn't give Miss Finney
all the cards she had made.

She didn't have to!

Dear Willaby,
Thank you for
the get-well
picture.

Miss Finney

Summary Questions

Willaby wanted Miss Finney to know that she liked her.

These questions will help you tell what Willaby did.

1. What did Willaby forget to put on her picture for Miss Finney?
2. Why do you think Willaby made so many cards for Miss Finney?
3. How did Willaby feel about going to school on the day that Miss Finney came back?
   Why did she feel that way?
4. Did Willaby need to put her name on her picture? Why?

The Reading and Writing Connection

What things do you think
Willaby will make for Miss Finney
if she gets sick again?

Tell how you think Miss Finney
would feel about them.

The words you see in the picture
may help you.

Miss Finney
decide
card
poem
picture

Johnny Drew a Monster

by Lilian Moore

Johnny drew a monster.
The monster chased him.
Just in time
Johnny erased him.

168

Who Helps Bear Cubs?

New bear cubs are so little.

They can't see well.

They can't get things to eat.

But they are cute!

When cubs are so little,
they do not go out.

The mother bear gives her cubs
all that they need.

Soon the cubs are not so little.
They go out with their mother.
Everything is new to the cubs!
They want to see everything.
The cubs have a good time
jumping, rolling, and playing.
Don't they look cute?

The mother bear is with her cubs
all the time.

She helps them find things to eat.

She helps them know all about
the things bears do.

Someday, when the cubs are big,
their mother will not need
to help them.

Summary Questions

The questions will help you tell about bear cubs.

1. Why do new cubs need help?
2. What does the mother bear do to help her cubs when they go out?
3. Someday the bear cubs will not need help. Why not?

The Reading and Writing Connection

Tell a story about three things that you think the cubs will do when they get big.

The words in the box will help you.

| their | cubs | play | fish | sleep |

Naming Words

The words in the box name
some animals you may find at a pond.

| turtles   ducks   fish |

Look at the picture.
Look at the naming words in the box.

Which animal name goes in each one
of these to tell about the picture?

1. There is one _____ in the pond.
2. There are two _____ in the pond.
3. There are three _____ in the pond.

The Five Silly Bears

The Five Silly Bears think
that one Silly Bear is lost.
Find out why they think so.

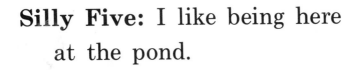

Silly Five: I like being here
    at the pond.

Silly Two: I do, too.
    We have had fun.
    But we came here to get some fish,
    and not one of us could get one.

Silly Five: Now it's time to go home.

Silly One: Yes, it's getting dark.
    It's so dark that I can't see
    all of us.

Silly Three: I know that I am here.
Do you think that one of us fell
into the pond?

Silly Four: Yes, I think so!

Silly Five: Well, I don't think so.
I'll count us and see if one of us
is lost.
Here I go.
One, two, three, four.

Silly Three: Oh, no!
There were five of us when we came
to the pond.
You have counted only four.

Silly Two: We have lost a Silly Bear!

Silly Four: Boohoo! Boohoo!
One Silly Bear fell into the pond.
What are we going to do?

Silly Three: Maybe you didn't count every bear, Silly Five.

Silly Five: But I did!

Silly Three: Well then, who fell in?

Silly One: I didn't.

Silly Two: Look, here comes Fox. We can ask Fox for help.

Silly Four: No one can help us.
   Boohoo! Boohoo!

Fox: Why are you crying, you Silly Bear?

Silly Four: One of us is lost, Fox.

Silly Three: We think that one of us
   fell into the pond.

Silly Five: When we came here,
   there were five Silly Bears.
   Now we can find only four of us.

Silly One: We have to find
the lost Silly Bear.

Silly Two: We have to fish
that Silly Bear out of the pond.

Fox: Who did the counting?

Silly Five: I did.

Fox: Let me see you count,
Silly Bear Five.

Silly Five: One, two, three, four.

Silly Four: See, Fox?
There are only four of us.
Boohoo! Boohoo!

Fox: Stop, Silly Bear Four!
There is nothing to cry about!

Silly Four: Nothing to cry about?
Why not?
Have you found the lost Silly Bear?

Fox: No one is lost.
Look, I will count.
One, two, three, four, five.

Silly Three: Five bears!
When Silly Five counted,
he counted only four bears.

Silly Five: Where did you find
the lost bear?
Did I forget someone?

Fox: You did forget someone, Silly Five.
When you counted, you did not
count yourself!

Silly Five: Oh, that was silly of me!

Silly One: Well, now that Fox showed
that we are all here, we can go home.

All the Bears: Thank you
for finding all of us, Fox.
Good-by!

Fox: Good-by, you Silly Bears.
And don't forget this, Silly Five.
When you count Silly Bears,
you need to count yourself, too!

Summary Questions

The Five Silly Bears had a problem. These questions will help you tell what they did about it.

1. Why did the Five Silly Bears think one of them was lost?

2. How did Silly Bear Five count to see if they were all there?

3. How did Fox help the Silly Bears?

4. What if one more Silly Bear was waiting for the Five Silly Bears to come home? What would the Five Silly Bears tell him about their day?

The Reading and Writing Connection

Tell a story about a time
when one of the Five Silly Bears
does get lost.

Tell how the Silly Bears
find out he is lost.

Then tell how the Silly Bears
and their friend Fox find the lost bear.

The words in the box will help you.

count	**five**	**four**	**every**
time	**crying**	**nothing**	

What Will Happen?

Have a good day, Pam.

Think about what will happen next.

1. Pam will go to the store.
2. Pam will go to school.

What helped you to know that Pam is going to school?

Here are some things that helped you.
Pam was taking books.
Gramps said, "Have a good day, Pam."

186

Read what is in this box.

> "We'll go to the pond
> after breakfast," said Dad to Lee.
> "We'll take our boat with us.
> We'll take some worms, too."

Where are Dad and Lee going?
1. They are going to the movies.
2. They are going fishing.

What helped you to know that Dad
and Lee are going fishing?

Thinking about both the boat
and the worms helped.

Thinking about the pond helped, too.

Were there any other things
that helped you?

Sometimes you can tell what
will happen next if you think about
what you have read and what you know.

Now read what is in this box.

Dad put a worm on Lee's fishing line.

Lee put the line into the pond.

Lee and Dad sat still.

Soon both of them saw something jump.

Then Lee's fishing line jumped.

What do you think happened next?
What helped you to know that?

Ira Sleeps Over

**story and
pictures by
Bernard Waber**

Ira is going
to sleep over
at Reggie's house.

Ira needs to decide
if he will take
his teddy bear.

If Ira takes
the bear, will Reggie
say that Ira is silly?

If Ira doesn't
take the bear, will he
miss it?

Find out what Ira
decides to do.

Ira
Sleeps
Over

by Bernard Waber

Part 1

I was going to sleep over
at Reggie's house.
It was going to be fun.

But I had a problem.
It was my sister who thought
of the problem.

She asked, "Are you taking
your teddy bear?"

"Taking my teddy bear!" I said.
"To Reggie's house?
No, I'm not taking my teddy bear."

And then she said, "How will it be
sleeping without your teddy bear?
Hmmmmmm?"

"It will be OK.
I'll like sleeping
without my teddy bear," I said.

But now she had me thinking
about it.
"What if I don't like sleeping
without my teddy bear?" I thought.
"Maybe I'll take him."

"Take him," said my mother.

"Take him," said my father.

"But Reggie will laugh," I said.

"He won't laugh," said my mother.

"He won't laugh," said my father.

"He'll laugh," said my sister.

I decided not to take my teddy bear.

After that I went to play
with Reggie.

Reggie said, "When you come
to my house, we are going
to have fun, fun, fun."

"Good," I said, "I can't wait."

"By the way," I asked, "what do
you think of teddy bears?"

But Reggie said nothing
about teddy bears.

"When you sleep over,
we'll tell stories," said Reggie.
"We'll tell ghost stories."

"Ghost stories?" I asked.

"Yes, ghost stories," said Reggie.

I thought about my teddy bear.

"Does your house get dark?" I asked.

"Uh-huh," said Reggie.

"Very dark?" I asked.

"Uh-huh," said Reggie.

"By the way," I asked, "what do you think of teddy bears?"

But then Reggie had to go home. "See you," said Reggie.

"See you," I said.
I decided to take
my teddy bear.

"Good," said my mother.

"Good," said my father.

But my sister said, "Will you tell
Reggie your teddy bear's name?
Did you think about how he
will laugh at a name like Tah Tah?"

"He won't ask," I said.

"He'll ask," she said.

I decided not to take Tah Tah.

199

Summary Questions

These questions will help you tell what Ira decided to do about taking Tah Tah to Reggie's house.

1. Why did Ira want to take Tah Tah?
2. What did Ira's family tell him to do?
3. What did Ira decide to do? Why?

The Reading and Writing Connection

Think of something Ira could do so Reggie won't laugh if he takes Tah Tah.
Draw a picture and tell about it.
The words in the box may help you.

family	sister	laugh
won't	sleep	night

200

Ira Sleeps Over

by Bernard Waber

Part 2

It was time to go to Reggie's house.

"Good night," said my mother.

"Good night," said my father.

"Sleep tight," said my sister.

I went over to Reggie's house.

That night we played
with everything in Reggie's room.

Then Reggie's father said,
"Bedtime!"

"Now?" asked Reggie.

"Now," said his father.
"Sleep tight."

We got into bed.

"Now we can tell ghost stories,"
said Reggie.

"Do you know one?" I asked.

"Uh-huh," said Reggie.
"Once there was this ghost
who lived in a big, dark house.
    And every night this ghost said,
Ooooh! Oooooooooh! Like that."

"This ghost would go looking
for someone to scare," said Reggie.

"And the ghost was very scary
to look at.

Oh, was it scary to look at!"

Reggie stopped.
"Are you scared?" he asked.

"Uh-huh, are you?" I asked.

"What?" asked Reggie.

"Are you scared?" I asked.

"Wait," said Reggie.
"I have to get something."

"What is it?" I asked.

"Oh, something," said Reggie.

Reggie got the something out.
The room was dark, but I
could see what he had.
It looked like a teddy bear.
I looked some more.
It *was* a teddy bear.

Reggie got back into bed.
"Now, about the ghost . . . " he said.

"Is that your teddy bear?" I asked.

"This teddy bear?" asked Reggie.

"Yes, that one," I said.

"Uh-huh," said Reggie.

"Do you sleep with it
all of the time?" I asked.

"Uh-huh," said Reggie.

"Does your teddy bear
have a name?" I asked.

"You won't laugh?" asked Reggie.

"No, I won't laugh," I said.

"It's Foo Foo," said Reggie.

"Foo Foo?" I asked.

"Uh-huh," said Reggie.

"I have to get something," I said.

"What do you have to get?" asked Reggie.

"Oh, something," I said.

I went back to my house.

"Ira!" everyone said.
"What are you
doing here?"

"I decided to take
Tah Tah," I said.

I went up
to my room.
I came back
with Tah Tah.

My sister said,
"Reggie will laugh."

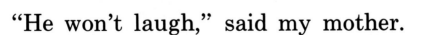

"He won't laugh," said my mother.

"He won't laugh," said my father.

"He won't laugh," I said.

I came back to Reggie's room.
"I have a teddy bear, too," I said.
"Do you want to know his name?"

I waited, but Reggie said nothing.
I looked at Reggie.
He was sleeping.

"Reggie!" I said.
"You have to tell the ghost story!"
But Reggie went on sleeping.

And after that —
There was nothing to do after that.

"Good night," I said to Tah Tah.
And I went to sleep, too.

Story Wrap-up

Summary Questions

Ira didn't want to be scared.

The questions will help you tell what he did so he wouldn't be scared.

1. What did Reggie do that was scary?
2. What makes you think that Reggie was scared?
3. Why do you think Ira decided to get his teddy bear?
4. What do you think Reggie will say when he finds out that Ira has a teddy bear?
5. Do you think that what Ira did will help the boys be good friends? Tell why or why not.

The Reading and Writing Connection

Ira and Reggie liked their teddy bears
very much.

Many other children have
teddy bears, too.

Make up a poem that tells why
so many children like their teddy bears.

The words in the box may help you.

scary	sleep	new	play
scare	big	little	

My Teddy Bear

by Marchette Chute

A teddy bear is a faithful friend.
You can pick him up at either end.
His fur is the color
    of breakfast toast,
And he's always there
    when you need him most.

Magazine Wrap-up

Do You Remember?

1. What were Willaby, the Silly Bears, and Ira each scared of?

2. You have read about three kinds of bears.
   Tell about each kind.

Willaby Makes a Drawing for Ira

If Willaby made a drawing
for Ira, what would it look like?
Make the drawing or tell about it.

Books to Enjoy

Gone Fishing by Earlene Long
Father and his little boy go fishing.
Find out who gets a big fish.

Little Bear by Else Minarik
Here are four good stories about
Little Bear and Mother Bear.

It's Not Easy Being a Bunny
by Marilyn Sadler
A rabbit wants to be a bear or a pig.
He wants to be anything but a rabbit!

216

Picture Dictionary

Aa

ask
What did you **ask**?

Bb

boat
The **boat** is on the pond.

boys
Lee and Dan are **boys.**

Cc

children
The **children** sing well.

count

Can you **count** the books?

crying

Tina was **crying.**

Dd

dark

It is **dark**
when I go to bed.

decide

Pam will **decide**
what to do.

Dd

draw
What can you **draw**?

Ee

eat
He will **eat** now.

Ff

family
This is my **family.**

five
Susan is **five.**

Hh

house
My **house** is red.

hungry
The **hungry** boy
had some soup.

Jj

jar
What can go in a **jar**?

Kk

key
Here is the **key** to the box.

Kk

kitchen
We make lunch
in the **kitchen.**

Ll

laugh
The silly bear
made Mary **laugh.**

listen
Listen for the cat.

Mm

money
Jed will count
his **money.**

Nn

night
I go to bed
at **night**.

Pp

paint
Put the red **paint** here.

picture
Ben put a dog
in the **picture**.

plant
Dad will **plant**
the tree.

Rr

room

I have a big bed
in my **room.**

Ss

said

"Come with me,"
she **said.**

sign

A word is
on the **sign.**

sleep

I **sleep** in a bed.

store
You can get fish
at the pet **store.**

street
Do not play
in the **street.**

swim
Can you see
the fish **swim**?

Tt

table
Lupe put the box
on the **table.**

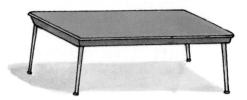

three
Alma can count to **three.**

tree
The cat is up the **tree.**

Ww

walk
We will **walk** there.

window
What do you see
out the **window?**

225

Read
Write
Listen
Speak

Read

Reading Unknown Words

When you come to a new word —
- Read to the end of the sentence.
- Think about what the words are saying.
- Think about the sounds for the letters.

Sounds You Know

b c d f g h j k l m n p r s t v w x y

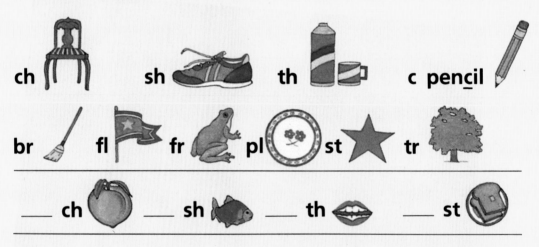

ch   sh   th   c pen<u>c</u>il

br   fl   fr   pl   st   tr

___ ch   ___ sh   ___ th   ___ st

short **a**    long **a**

can   am   make   take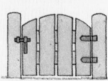

New Sounds

kn sc  ___ ck

 ___ y

More New Sounds – Vowels

short **e**

red   let   went

long **e**

feel   these   we

short **i**

his   with   if

long **i**

line   time   five

short **o**

stop   hot   got

long **o**

home   nose   poke

short **u**

cut   run   up

long **u**

cute

Write

The Writing Process

1 Prewriting

- Think of some story ideas.
- Make a list.
- Choose one idea.
- Draw a picture.
- Tell about your picture.

231

❷ Write a First Draft

● Make sentences to tell your story.

③ Revise

- Read the story.
- Talk about the story.
- Tell more.

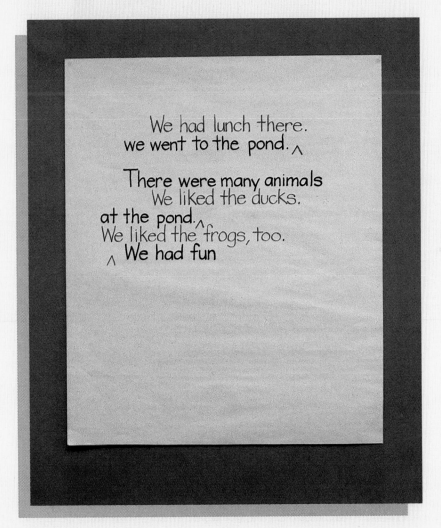

We had lunch there.
we went to the pond. ∧

There were many animals
We liked the ducks.
at the pond. ∧
We liked the frogs, too.
∧ We had fun

233

④ Proofread

- Look at the story again.
- Fix any mistakes.

⑤ Publish

- Make a final copy
  for everyone to see.

Our Pond Trip
We went to the pond.
We had lunch there.
There were many animals
at the pond.
We liked the ducks.
We liked the frogs, too.
We had fun.

Listen and Speak

Listening

Speaking

Credits